STEAM HERITAGE
1972–1985

A PICTORIAL TRIBUTE

I would like to dedicate this book to BEN, in recognition of his love of steam trains.

STEAM HERITAGE
1972–1985

A PICTORIAL TRIBUTE

DAVID KNAPMAN

PEN & SWORD
TRANSPORT

AN IMPRINT OF PEN & SWORD BOOKS LTD.
YORKSHIRE – PHILADELPHIA

First published in Great Britain in 2023 by
Pen and Sword Transport
An imprint of
Pen & Sword Books Ltd.
Yorkshire - Philadelphia

ISBN 978 1 52679 253 2

A CIP catalogue record for this book is available from the British Library.

Typeset by SJmagic DESIGN SERVICES, India.
Printed and bound in India by Replika Press Pvt. Ltd.

Pen & Sword Books Ltd incorporates the imprints of Pen & Sword Books Archaeology, Atlas, Aviation, Battleground, Discovery, Family History, History, Maritime, Military, Naval, Politics, Railways, Select, Transport, True Crime, Fiction, Frontline Books, Leo Cooper, Praetorian Press, Seaforth Publishing, Wharncliffe and White Owl.

For a complete list of Pen & Sword titles please contact

PEN & SWORD BOOKS LIMITED
47 Church Street, Barnsley, South Yorkshire, S70 2AS, England
E-mail: enquiries@pen-and-sword.co.uk
Website: www.pen-and-sword.co.uk

or

PEN AND SWORD BOOKS
1950 Lawrence Rd, Havertown, PA 19083, USA
E-mail: Uspen-and-sword@casematepublishers.com
Website: www.penandswordbooks.com

CONTENTS

INTRODUCTION

By the time this book is published, it will be over fifty years since the main line steam revival began in October 1971 with the return to steam by 6000 *King George V*, thanks to the efforts of Peter Prior and the willingness of the British Railways Board to allow a week-long railtour to proceed. On this historic tour, the 'King' travelled from Hereford to Tyseley via Severn Tunnel Junction for the first stage of the tour, followed by Birmingham to Kensington Olympia and then to Swindon, before finally returning to Hereford after 525 miles of reliable performance.

So, just over three years since main line steam operation in the UK had finished, *King George V* had led the way for steam's return to the main line. This, of course, is not the whole story in that the preservation movement was developing and beginning to mature as more preserved railways opened throughout the country. The developments taking place fifty years ago, and subsequently, are forming their own history, and it was with this in mind that John Scott-Morgan of Pen & Sword invited me to write two books covering the steam heritage scene. The first period to be covered is 1972 to 1985 and the second 1986 to 2000, during which times main line steam travel and preserved railways developed and matured into the steam operations we saw as we entered the twenty-first century.

This book contains colour pictures from my collection of large format colour slides taken during 1972 to 1985. The style of the book will be similar to my previous books published by Pen & Sword and includes 200 pictures supported by informative captions. These previous books have been set out in British Railways regional format, but

after 1971 main line locomotives could be seen outside their customary travelling routes. It was therefore agreed that this book would be set out chronologically.

An analysis of the available slides for 1972 to 1985 reveals at least ninety different locomotives to display. It must be mentioned that a number of these locomotives had emerged from the Barry Island scrapyard to be restored by numerous volunteers as preservation progressed. Their enormous work cannot be overestimated, because without those efforts, there would be no history to record. This is a salute to the volunteer movement.

The earlier years in this book will inevitably be a bit thin on the ground, reflecting the newness of the movement as well as making allowances for my early years of marriage and a new family life. It is all a matter of balance, which is something that chartered accountants are supposed to take in their stride!

The large format pictures were taken initially using a folding Agfa Isolette II and later with twin lens reflex Mamiya cameras, coupled with a selection of lenses. The Mamiyas were heavy to carry but were a pleasure to use. They required careful single shot photography, the complete antithesis of digital multi shot cameras today.

Once more, I am pleased to express my grateful thanks to John Scott-Morgan, Janet Brookes, Paul Wilkinson and the Pen & Sword Team, whose patience and support is a delight.

Further grateful thanks are due to Jenifer and David Alison, whose review of my writing has helped enormously in bringing this book to fruition.

I hope *Steam Heritage 1972 to 1985* stirs the memory banks of readers and gives them the pleasure of recalling the events of these years. If you have comments you would like to pass on, please do so via Pen & Sword. Thank you for your interest and support.

The reader will find reference to a large number of railway companies, named trains, and preserved railways in this book. To save space and repetition, the first mention of these will show their name in full, but subsequent appearances will just show their initials (see the Glossary at the end of the book).

David Knapman.
Woburn,
March 2023

CHAPTER 1

1972 TO 1974: EARLY DAYS

In these formative years, only a few visits were made to the lineside or to preserved railways. Personal budgets of the day did not run to a multitude of railtours and so the early years of my photography really mirrored the growth of steam activity in the UK. The motive power observed in these years was in the main of Great Western Railway origin, supplemented by Pacific locomotives of the London and North Eastern Railway. Photographs may not always be of moving subjects as it is not possible to have the best of both worlds when travelling on trains. Interestingly, the 75th anniversary, July 1972, issue of *Railway Magazine* carried a list of twenty-three steam locomotives approved to run on British Railways, of which ten were Great Western Railway; seven London Midland & Scottish Railway; three London North Eastern Railway; two British Railways and one representative of the Southern Railway, which was 35028 *Clan Line*. In 1972, twelve steam railtours were run, with that number doubling in 1973, whilst 1974 reverted to a quieter fourteen trains. Early days indeed.

My first railtour in preservation was on the *Steam Safari* when the motive power was provided by 'A4' 4-6-2 4498 *Sir Nigel Gresley*. The 'A4' entered service in November 1937 and after withdrawal in 1966, the A4 Locomotive Society purchased 4498 and arranged for an overhaul of the locomotive at Crewe. British Rail announced a steam ban on 12 August 1968 and the *Steam Safari* was the first tour for 4498, following the lifting of the ban. 4498 is seen at a photographic stop at Haltwhistle, en route from Carlisle to Newcastle. 19 June 1972.

A first lineside effort captured 'King' 4-6-0 6000 *King George V* hauling a Hereford to Shrewsbury special train at Moreton-on-Lugg. The tour was sponsored by the Great Western Society, using 6000 from its then base at Bulmers, Hereford. It ran nearly two million miles in thirty-five years of railway service and was withdrawn in 1962 for the National Collection. The 'King' is now a static exhibit at Swindon's STEAM museum. 24 June 1973.

On the same day as 6000's special train working, the GWS sponsored a second tour when their 'Modified Hall' 4-6-0 6998 *Burton Agnes Hall* hauled its first main line train in preservation. The route was Didcot, Worcester, Hereford and return to Worcester. 6998 was serviced at Bulmers, Hereford, which is the location of this photograph. It had worked the final steam service between Oxford and Banbury for BR's Western Region, before withdrawal in December 1965. The 'Hall' is now a static exhibit at GWS, Didcot. 24 June 1973.

Also present at Bulmers' depot was GWR '57xx' Pannier Tank 5786 in GWR livery. 5786 was sold by BR to London Transport in 1958, when it was renumbered L92. Subsequently, the Worcester Locomotive Society bought it in 1969 and it was based at Bulmers until 1993. This Pannier Tank is now on loan to the South Devon Railway. 24 June 1973.

Flying Scotsman Enterprises arranged the *Great Northern* railtour for 6 April 1974, which commemorated the first reunion of 'A3' 4472 *Flying Scotsman* and 'Castle' 4079 *Pendennis Castle* since the Wembley Exhibition in 1925. 4079 was withdrawn from BR service in June 1964 and went into the ownership of Bill McAlpine and John Gretton. The 'Castle' provided motive power for the Newport to Shrewsbury leg of the tour. 4079 is pictured at Shrewsbury, prior to turning on the triangle. 6 April 1974.

The *Great Northern* railtour was literally seconds from departure time at Shrewsbury behind 'A3' 4-6-2 4472 *Flying Scotsman*, when the opportunity to photograph 4472 and 4079 together suddenly materialised, although 4079 appears to be a little camera shy. I did not miss the train. 4472 was owned by Bill McAlpine at this time. 6000 *King George V* was stand-by locomotive, if needed, but the rostered motive power worked their turns satisfactorily. 6 April 1974.

Bulmers Hereford held an open day on 14 April 1974, when it hosted two visiting locomotives, one of which was 'Castle' 4-6-0 4079 *Pendennis Castle,* none the worse for its exertions on the North and West route the previous weekend. The 'Castle' is carrying the *Bristolian* headboard, an enticing prospect. 4079 is currently being restored at GWS Didcot. 14 April 1974.

The flagship locomotive at Bulmers, Hereford was, of course, 'King' 4-6-0 6000 *King George V* proudly sporting its commemorative bell from the 1927 visit to the USA. 6000 is surrounded by many admirers. 14 April 1974.

A visit to the Torbay Railway found GWR '45XX' 2-6-2T 4588 at the head of a Kingswear bound train at Churston. 4588 is in charge of a set of chocolate and cream liveried coaches as it enters Churston Station bunker first. The 2-6-2T was withdrawn from BR service in July 1962 from Plymouth Laira shed and went to Barry scrapyard. It was the eleventh locomotive to leave Barry, in October 1970, and worked on the Buckfastleigh and Kingswear lines until it moved to Peak Rail in 2015. 9 September 1974.

The Midlander main line tour provided the final event for 1974. The train included a journey on the Severn Valley Railway headed by '5MT' 4-6-0 45110. On the main line, 'King' 6000 *King George V* was at the head of the train for the Shrewsbury to Hereford section, but provided a disappointing performance. By contrast, 'Jubilee' 4-6-0 5690 *Leander* was very energetic between Hereford and Oxford, especially on the climb to Colwall. Photo opportunities were limited and so 6000 is shown at Shrewsbury prior to working to Hereford. 5 October 1974.

CHAPTER 2

1975: AN ANNIVERSARY YEAR

975 was an eventful year, domestically and from a railway interest point of view. Our first daughter, Alex, was born and that would mean matters at home rightly having priority.

The railway preservation scene was continuing to develop and its maturing process was to be splendidly demonstrated in the Rail 150 Exhibition Steam Cavalcade at Shildon, County Durham, using the route of the Stockton and Darlington Railway from Shildon to Heighington.

Fortunately, I was able to witness the Cavalcade and the event will form a large part of this chapter. All the Cavalcade pictures were taken on 31 August 1975. A Devon holiday also enabled some preserved railway activity.

In 1975, twenty two locomotives were approved for main line running and the Steam Locomotive Operators Association was formed to co-ordinate the programme of steam hauled specials on BR. A further step in the maturing process.

Ex-GWR '14XX' 0-4-2T 1450 is pictured at Buckfastleigh on the Dart Valley Railway, now known as the South Devon Railway. It was withdrawn from Exmouth Junction shed in April 1965 and was purchased by the DVR. In 1963, 1450 participated in the *West Countryman* railtour, by hauling a train of brake vans from Tiverton Junction to Hemyock and return. This super locomotive is currently based at the Severn Valley Railway and is awaiting refurbishment following expiry of its boiler certificate. 15 July 1975.

1450 is seen here making a gentle departure from Buckfastleigh en route for Totnes. Note the Devon Belle observation car immediately behind the engine. 15 July 1975.

Above left: This narrow gauge locomotive No. 1 *Woolwich* was built by Avonside in 1915 and was purchased by the Bicton Gardens Railway from Woolwich Arsenal. The unusual gauge for the railway is eighteen inches. *Woolwich* is shown at Bicton Gardens station. It provided our daughter's first steam hauled journey. 16 July 1975.

Above right: A brief interlude at the East Somerset Railway revealed BR '9F' 2-10-0 92203 *Black Prince* in the shed at Cranmore. 92203 was built at Swindon in 1959 and withdrawn from service in November 1967. The '9F' was purchased direct from BR by the artist David Shepherd and moved initially to the Longmoor Military Railway. In 1973, 92203 moved to Cranmore and subsequently ownership changed to the North Norfolk Railway, where the locomotive now resides. Presumably the 82H shedplate signified Cranmore. 19 July 1975.

A group of us decided to be present at the Rail 150 Cavalcade on 31 August 1975, an important anniversary event and quoted as being an 'Exhibition of Locomotives, Rolling Stock, and other relics on a scale unlikely to be repeated'. The grand steam Cavalcade included over thirty steam locomotives including a working replica of *Locomotion No.1*. We joined an LNER Society railtour leaving Euston at 23.35 and arriving at Lancaster soon after 07.00, where road coaches were ready to take passengers to Shildon by 09.45, in time for the two hour Cavalcade, which started at 14.00. The gathering of locomotives is depicted here, at a distance, but this was as close as we were permitted. 31 August 1975.

Colour pictures of the Cavalcade were restricted by my budget to a few chosen subjects. Taking photographs under covered stands, into strong sunlight, was not straightforward. Clearly photography was not uppermost in the organisers' minds. This photograph of 'K1' 2-6-0 2005 demonstrates the facility available; the awning did however keep the direct sunlight off the camera lens. 2005 was built in 1949 and spent her working life in the North East of England, before being withdrawn in December 1967. The 'K1' was privately purchased in 1968 as is based at the North Yorkshire Moors Railway. It is a regular performer on *The Jacobite* train in the West Highlands.

Former LNER, Gresley designed, 'D49' 4-4-0 246 *Morayshire* passes the covered stands. 246 is blowing off steam from the safety valves. The 'D49' was withdrawn from Hawick shed in July 1961 and purchased for preservation. It is now owned by the National Museum of Scotland and is currently under overhaul.

Representing the GWR is 'Modified Hall' 4-6-0 6960 *Raveningham Hall*. Built at Swindon in 1944, 6960 was withdrawn from Oxford shed in June 1964 and sent to Barry Island where it rested for eight years, before moving to Carnforth for restoration. Later it moved to the SVR and is now owned by Locomotive Services Ltd.

Cavalcade exhibit 11 was Sir Nigel Gresley's 'V2' 2-6-2 4771 *Green Arrow* looking resplendent in LNER livery. 4771 finished its service at King's Cross shed in August 1962 and was retained as part of the National Collection. It was returned to steam in 1973 and worked on the main line and various preserved lines until 2008.

A delight to see in the Cavalcade. Patrick Stirling's 'Eight Foot' Single locomotive Great Northern Railway No. 1. It was previously steamed in 1938, when special trains were run on the LNER. Subsequent to this appearance, the locomotive was seen in steam on the Great Central Railway in 1982 and some of its activity will be shown later. In the Cavalcade, No. 1 was hauled by 'A4' 4498 *Sir Nigel Gresley* as the Stirling Single was not in steam.

Another GNR locomotive in the form of 'C1' 4-4-2 990 *Henry Oakley* was built at Doncaster in 1898. The Atlantic ceased work in 1937 and is also part of the National Collection. It was most fitting that 990 was in steam for this event.

Exhibit 20 was the London & North Western Railway 'Precedent' 2-4-0 790 *Hardwicke*, well known for its energetic exploits in the railway races from London to Aberdeen, achieving an average speed of 67mph between Crewe and Carlisle on 22 August 1895. A remarkable effort, especially with so little cab protection. 790 was last steamed in 1980.

Hardwicke was followed by Midland Railway 'Compound' 4-4-0 1000, built in 1902, resplendent in crimson lake livery. 1000 was withdrawn from ordinary service in 1951, and was restored to working order in the early 1960's. It had a further period in steam in the 1980's, including work on the Settle to Carlisle line.

4-4-0 1000 appropriately preceded LMS 'Jubilee' 4-6-0 5690 *Leander*. These two locomotives were to work together in Yorkshire, replicating a regular double heading combination once seen regularly. 5690 was withdrawn in March 1964 from Bristol, Barrow Road, and despatched to Barry Island. It was purchased privately, restored at Derby works and worked on the main line in the 1980's. It is currently owned by Chris Beet and is based at Carnforth for use in main line traffic.

LMS 'Princess Royal' Pacific 6201 *Princess Elizabeth* presented its customary elegant and immaculate appearance. This 1933 built Stanier designed locomotive holds the record for the longest and fastest non-stop steam hauled train when it travelled between Euston and Glasgow at an average speed of 70.1mph in November 1936. The Princess Elizabeth Society acquired 6201 from BR in 1962, and it is currently based at Carnforth awaiting repairs.

A very pleasing surprise was seeing Wantage Tramway 0-4-0WT No. 5 *Shannon.* No. 5 was built in 1857 for the Sandy and Potton Railway. Later, *Shannon* was a works shunter at Crewe for the LNWR, before being sold to the Wantage Tramway, which closed in 1945. Having been exhibited at Wantage Road Station, *Shannon* then moved to the GWS at Didcot, where it is now a static exhibit.

The Cavalcade would not be complete without seeing one of the once ubiquitous 'Terrier' 0-6-0T's of the London, Brighton & South Coast Railway. Here 636 *Fenchurch* sparkles in the afternoon sun as it passes the spectators' enclosures. Built in 1872, it ran over 1.1 million miles before ceasing service in 1964. It is now based at the Bluebell Railway and is awaiting overhaul.

Maunsell designed 'S15' 4-6-0 841 *Greene King* followed next. This Southern Railway mixed traffic locomotive was built in 1936 and was in service until 1964. It then went to Barry Island for eight years before moving to the NYMR, where its boiler was latterly used on sister locomotive 825.

Last but not least of the cavalcade photographs shows 'Merchant Navy' Pacific 35028 *Clan Line*. This Bulleid designed and subsequently rebuilt 4-6-2 was purchased direct from BR by the Merchant Navy Locomotive Preservation Society and has been a reliable main line performer since the 1970s, always presented in immaculate condition. A worthy attendee at the 1975 Cavalcade.

CHAPTER 3

1976 & 1977: PACIFIC POWER AND A FAREWELL

Colour photography was not the first choice in 1976 as my diary notes record that the combination of LNWR 2-4-0 790 *Hardwicke* and Midland 'Compound' 4-4-0 seen at Bell Busk were captured on black and white film. So it was not until the autumn of 1976 that colour film reappeared at Carnforth and on the Ravenglass and Eskdale Railway, followed by a three locomotive tour on the North & West route in October. 1976 was the centenary year for the Settle & Carlisle Railway and various locations were visited, but curiously steam trains were not permitted over the line in 1976 and 1977.

1977 saw the farewell to 4079 *Pendennis Castle* at Didcot and a particularly enjoyable tour in the North with LNER Pacifics and 'V2' 2-6-2 *Green Arrow*. Interesting times.

On the RER, 2-8-2 *River Mite* is entering Irton Road station past 2-6-2 *Northern Rock* as the latter waits for the road for Ravenglass. The 2-8-2 was built in 1966 by H. Clarkson & Son, whilst *Northern Rock* is a product of the R&ER works at Ravenglass. 8 September 1976.

A rainy visit to Steamtown, Carnforth found ex-GWR 'Modified Hall' 4-6-0 6960 *Raveningham Hall* in steam, alongside the coaling tower, a unique feature to survive at this location. 11 September 1976.

Without a breath of steam in sight, Ribblehead Viaduct, in its centenary year, stands proudly, awaiting a very active future, thanks to those people who had the vision to save the Settle to Carlisle line. 15 September 1976.

The MNLPS promoted the 'Marches Merchantman' railtour on 2 October 1976, when three main line locomotives were employed. 'Princess Royal' 4-6-2 6201 *Princess Elizabeth* worked from Hereford to Shrewsbury, where she is pictured, before a locomotive change.

The *Marches Merchantman* is about to be heading northwards from Shrewsbury behind 'King' 4-6-0 6000 *King George V* bound for Chester, where 6000 will be replaced by 'Merchant Navy' Pacific 35028 *Clan Line* for the return to Hereford. 2 October 1976.

On the final stage of the *Marches Merchantman* tour, 35028 *Clan Line* is pictured at Ruabon, during a photostop. Note for the reader: photography in the early years of railtours was more relaxed and some photographs may appear to be taken from positions unacceptable today. Stewards were also alert to the proceedings. 2 October 1976.

The North & West route was in business for railtours in Spring 1977 when the Midland & Great Northern Joint Railway Society ran the *Cathedrals Express* from Hereford to Chester and return. At the lineside near All Stretton, 'King' 4-6-0 6000 *King George V* is working hard on the climb to Church Stretton with the return train from Chester. The sun appeared in good time to illuminate the train nicely. 23 April 1977.

The SVR also sponsored a special train on the same route and using the same locomotives as the MGNJRPS. The light was fading fast as the second train approached All Stretton behind 'Princess Royal' 4-6-2 6201 *Princess Elizabeth* working hard towards Church Stretton, with the *Severn Valley Limited* using SVR vintage coaching stock. 23 April 1977.

1977 saw the export of one of our most famous locomotives, namely 'Castle' 4-6-0 4079 *Pendennis Castle*. Built at Swindon in 1924, 4079 was, in 1925, in comparative trials with Gresley Pacifics from the LNER, and at that time 4079 outperformed the Pacifics. In 1977, 4079 was sold to the Hamersley Iron Company in Australia, but thankfully was returned to the UK in 2000 and has now returned to steam at GWS Didcot. Here 4079 is depicted leaving Didcot yard after servicing, prior to returning to Saltley. 29 May 1977.

With the sun glinting on 4079's firebox, *Pendennis Castle* makes an explosive start from Didcot as she takes the *Great Western Envoy* train back to Birmingham. Note the red circular Hamersley Iron symbol on the centre splasher and the vintage carriage with balcony, behind the tender. 29 May 1977.

More Pacifics. The LNER society sponsored a railtour based on Steamtown at Carnforth in Autumn 1977. The railtour net was clearly spreading and three locomotives were in use for the 'North Eastern Jubilee' between Carnforth and York. Two trains were necessary and we were allocated seats in the second train which facilitated some useful photography at Carnforth. Here 'A4' 4-6-2 4498 *Sir Nigel Gresley* is near the coaling tower. 'A3' 4-6-2 4472 *Flying Scotsman* is behind the 'A4'. 17 September 1977.

'A3' 4-6-2 4472 *Flying Scotsman* is under the coaling tower at Carnforth, with just a few onlookers. 4472 was designed by Nigel Gresley and built in 1923 at Doncaster as an 'A1' Pacific. It was later modified to an 'A3' Pacific with improved valve arrangements; this was one of the resulting consequences of the trials against the GWR 'Castles'. At the time of this photograph, 4472 was in LNER apple green livery and sported a single chimney. Its base was then Carnforth and it was then owned by Flying Scotsman Enterprises.17 September 1977.

LNER 'B1' 4-6-0 1306 *Mayflower* was also in steam, providing local rides in the yard at Carnforth. The 'B1' was not approved for main line work at the time but gave much interest on the day. 1306 is now owned by David Buck. 17 September 1977.

Train one of the *North Eastern Jubilee* departed for York behind 'A4' 4498 *Sir Nigel Gresley* and in this picture, it is taking the route for Wennington from Carnforth. A useful view is provided by the overbridge. 17 September 1977.

'A3' 4-6-2 4472 *Flying Scotsman* is at the Wennington photostop, heading the second train of the *North Eastern Jubilee,* bound for York. 17 September 1977.

A golden opportunity at Leeds City Station to capture the 'A3' and 'A4' pacifics together. My notes record that this tour was excellent, especially the return run from Leeds to Carnforth as we were in the front coach behind the 'A4'. 17 September 1977.

The final member of the tour trio, 'V2' 2-6-2 4771 *Green Arrow,* is looking immaculate at York prior to returning the train to Leeds. 4771 was built in 1936 at Doncaster and was named after the LNER fast freight service. The 'V2's were at home on express passenger and freight services as mixed traffic locomotives. 4771 was returned to steam in 1973 and worked the first steam train for ten years over the Settle to Carlisle line in 1978. At present, the 'V2' has a cracked cylinder block and has not steamed since 2008. 17 September 1977

CHAPTER 4

1978 & 1979: PRESERVED LINES AND NEW MOTIVE POWER

Having moved to an older house in 1977, my steam activities in 1978 and 1979 were rather curtailed by the need to renovate rooms and build a garage, as well as needing to commute to London to further my career at a new accounting firm. In 1978, we were blessed with the arrival of our second daughter Angie, so never a dull moment. However, some visits to preserved railways and participation in a couple of railtours provided much interest, especially as fresh locomotives were coming on stream. *Green Arrow* opened the Settle & Carlisle line to steam once more and over twenty railtours were agreed for 1978, with BR starting to promote their own steam excursions, now that steam was permitted to continue on the main line until 1985.

A visit to the formative GCR in May 1978 revealed that 1936 built Hunslet 0-6-0T saddle tank No. 4 *Robert Nelson* was motive power for the day. Main line power was not available for that visit but would soon follow. No. 4 was the first locomotive to steam for the preserved GCR. Note the sleepers on the bufferbeam, which remained there all day. Loughborough. 27 May 1978.

Signs of things to come, with Stanier '5MT' 4-6-0 5231 peeping out from under the bridge at Loughborough shed. The GCR was the first preservation home for 5231, until it found main line activity in 2005. It is now part of the Locomotive Services Ltd fleet. 27 May 1978.

In early summer 1978, a visit to the SVR proved to be most worthwhile with journeys behind GWR 'Manor' 7819 *Hinton Manor*, '4MT' 2-6-4T 80079 and 'Jinty' 0-6-0T 47383. It was interesting to record early restoration projects and this photograph shows another 'Manor' 4-6-0 7812 *Erlestoke Manor* at Bewdley in the process of being rebuilt from Barry Island condition to be steamed in 1979. 3 June 1978.

Also in the course of restoration at Bewdley was GWR '28XX' 2-8-0 2857, which had been rescued from Barry scrapyard after resting there for twelve years. 2857 was built at Swindon in 1918 and soon became a hard working member of the SVR fleet; its current boiler certificate expired in 2021. 3 June 1978.

At Bewdley, *Hinton Manor* awaits departure to Foley Park, then the furthest reach of the SVR before accessing Kidderminster. 7819 spent six and a half years at Barry before coming to the SVR, where it was returned to steam in 1977. It was a pleasure to see 7819 in action, having experienced its work on the *Cambrian Coast Express* in 1964. 3 June 1978.

Another SVR stalwart is '4MT' 2-6-4T 80079 pictured here at Bewdley. It was the thirteenth locomotive to leave Barry scrapyard and used to be a regular performer on the Fenchurch Street to Southend services. It has not been steamed for some while, as it is withdrawn with boiler deficiencies. 3 June 1978.

The Gresley designed 'K4' 2-6-0 3442 *The Great Marquess* was built in 1937 for the West Highland Line from Glasgow to Fort William and on to Mallaig. It was withdrawn from BR service in December 1961 and purchased by Viscount Garnock for overhaul and restoration to LNER livery. After working various railtour assignments until 1967, the 2-6-0 was stored until it went to the SVR in 1972. It is pictured at Arley awaiting further restoration. 3 June 1978.

'7MT' 4-6-2 70000 *Britannia* is in steam at Bridgnorth on the SVR. Built in 1951 and withdrawn from Newton Heath shed in 1966, 70000 was to have been part of the National Collection, but 70013 was selected instead. *Britannia* was purchased by the East Anglian Locomotive Preservation Society in 1970 and it moved to the SVR in April 1971. 70000 was returned to steam in May 1978 and is photographed here just after restoration. Note the white cab roof, and the nameplates have yet to be fitted. 3 June 1978.

All these locomotives are in steam, at Bridgnorth, SVR. From left to right are: 'Jinty' 0-6-0T 47383, '7MT' 4-6-2 70000 *Britannia*, '4MT' 2-6-4T 80079, and 'Manor' 4-6-0 7819 *Hinton Manor*. The preservation movement is developing well. 3 June 1978.

Before we leave the SVR, here is another view of '4MT' 2-6-4T 80079 approaching Arley station, with a Bridgnorth service. The short train will not tax the locomotive particularly. Note the lower quadrant signals directing the route. 3 June 1978.

An autumn holiday in Norfolk enabled a visit to the NNR with the prospect of seeing the 'J15' 0-6-0 in steam. As the picture shows, this was not to be, as it was under repair. 564 came to the NNR in 1967 and was returned to steam in 1977. Clearly further work was needed when the 'Little Goods' was seen at Sheringham. 17 September 1978.

The stalwart motive power of the *Wandering 1500* railtour of 5 October 1963 rests at Sheringham pending restoration. The unique inside cylinder 'B12' 4-6-0 61572 is in clean BR livery and the cab is open to visitors. The 'B12' also came to the NNR in 1967, but it was not steamed until 1995. 17 September 1978.

The Fenman railtour was sponsored by the 6000 Locomotive Association with 'Castle' 4-6-0 7029 *Clun Castle* as motive power from Hereford to Chester and 6000 *King George V* on return. Sadly the 'King' failed with a hot axle box, so steam operated in one direction only. 7029 was built at Swindon in May 1950 and was withdrawn in 1965, being purchased for preservation in 1966 by Patrick Whitehouse. It sports a four row superheater and double chimney and was a high speed performer on the Ian Allan railtour between Plymouth and Bristol on 9 May 1964. Here the 'Castle' is pictured at Ruabon during a photographic stop. 7 October 1978.

'Castle' 4-6-0 7029 *Clun Castle* is at Chester awaiting departure on the *Marches Venturer* railtour, which was run in conjunction with the 'Fenman'. 7029 is framed by part of the station structure, with welcome sunshine illuminating the locomotive. 7 October 1978.

7029 is heading away from Chester, with the *Marches Venturer* train, towards Hereford. The locomotive is currently owned by 7029 Clun Castle Ltd and is based at Tyseley. It returned to main line activity in 2019 after an extensive overhaul. 7 October 1978.

1978 activities were rounded off by travelling on the *Yorkshire Ranger* railtour sponsored by the 6000 Locomotive Association and the MGNJRPS. The first part of the steam section was from York to Harrogate, Leeds and return to York, managed by the immaculate 'V2' 2-6-2 4771 *Green Arrow*, seen during a photostop at Harrogate. 11 November 1978.

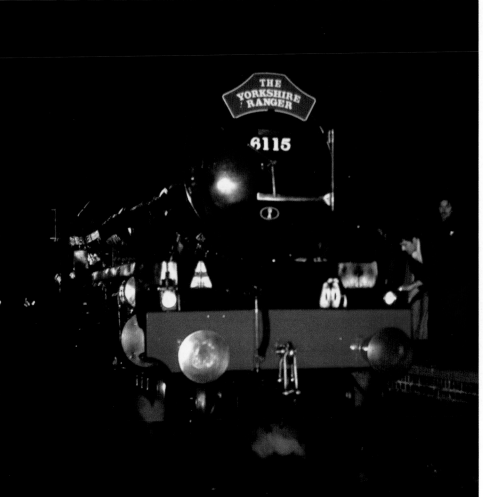

The *Yorkshire Ranger* participants were very much looking forward to the second stage of the tour, which would take them from York to Sheffield and on to Guide Bridge via Chinley. The motive power for this section was rebuilt 'Royal Scot' 4-6-0 6115 *Scots Guardsman,* freshly turned out in 1946 LMS black livery with straw and maroon lining. The only daylight opportunity for photographs was at York when fog descended to blight the picture. 11 November 1978.

The *Yorkshire Ranger* had a water stop at Sheffield, which enabled nocturnal photographs. 6115 had been withdrawn from BR service in January 1966 and was then purchased by Mr Bob Bill, with restoration work taking place at the Keighley and Worth Valley Railway. The level of mechanical restoration was only sufficient for haulage of two railtours, before a fresh BR ruling about boiler examination and restoration came into force. *Scots Guardsman* is now a magnificent performer as part of the West Coast Railways fleet. 11 November 1978.

A 1979 visit to the Midland Railway Centre at Butterley found LMS 'Princess Royal' 4-6-2 6203 *Princess Margaret Rose* on display. 6203 was the first of the production series of the class and entered traffic in July 1935. After nearly one and a half million miles in service 6203 was withdrawn in October 1962. In April 1963, it was purchased by Butlins, refurbished at Crewe and then transferred to Pwllheli holiday camp, her home for the next twelve years. In 1975, the Pacific was relocated to the MRC and in 1988 became the property of Brell Ewart. By 1990, it had been restored to main line duties, which lasted until April 1996. 6203 has been a static exhibit ever since. 26 August 1979.

The MRC had on display two of the National Collection locomotives. 1866-built Kirtley designed 2-4-0 158A is shown here, displaying its MR crimson lake livery, outside frames and outside coupled cranks. 158A survived in service until August 1947 and after display in a temporary museum in Leicester, moved to Butterley in June 1975. 26 August 1979.

The S.W. Johnson designed 4-2-2 673 for the MR was also on external display at Butterley. These elegant single driving wheel locomotives were nicknamed 'Spinners', and 673 was built in 1897 as number 118, being renumbered 673 in 1907. The 'Spinner' accompanied the Kirtley 2-4-0 in its travels before moving to Butterley in June 1975. 26 August 1979.

Another view of the 'Spinner' with the splendid livery slightly illuminated by weak sunshine. 673 is part of the National Collection and is now exhibited at York Railway Museum. It was a pleasure to see the MR locomotives outside. 26 August 1979.

Located at Butterley is 'Jinty' 0-6-0T 16440 (BR number 47357). This Fowler designed locomotive was built by the North British Locomotive Co Ltd for the LMS in 1926 and spent most of its working life at Willesden and Edge Hill. 47357 was withdrawn in December 1966, purchased by Derby Corporation in July 1970, and steamed in June 1973. It is shown here in unauthentic crimson lake livery as 16440. 26 August 1979.

The final railway activity for 1979 involved lineside observation of the *Leander Enterprise* railtour planned by Leander Locomotive Ltd on behalf of SLOA. The tour was steam hauled from Carnforth to Leeds and Harrogate, and on to York for the return to Leeds. 'Jubilee' 4-6-0 5690 *Leander* is seen in glorious sunshine at Bell Busk, heading for Skipton. 20 October 1979.

5690 *Leander* was joined by MR 'Compound' 4-4-0 1000 for part of the *Leander Enterprise* railtour and here the classic combination is seen heading for Harrogate near Weeton. Regrettably, the location was on the wrong side of the sunlight from a photographic point of view, but the double heading is nevertheless worthy of record. 20 October 1979.

Now in sole charge of the *Leander Enterprise,* 5690 crosses to the Leeds line at Church Fenton as the low sunshine picks out the LMS livery of the 4-6-0, heading away from York. 20 October 1979.

CHAPTER 5

1980: FAREWELL VINTAGE CARRIAGES AND WELCOME CUMBRIAN EXPRESSES

After a quiet year in 1979, 1980 reflected the ever growing steam scene and provided a great deal of interest, particularly with the emergence of the *Cumbrian Mountain Express* and the *Cumbrian Coast Express* both of which remain active currently. Steam was now well established over the Settle to Carlisle line, and 'Duchess'

46229 *Duchess of Hamilton* and 'Castle' 5051 *Drysllwyn Castle* returned to the main line. 1980 was the year for celebrating 'Rocket 150' by re-enacting the Rainhill Trials. Unfortunately, I was unable to be present. By 1980, 1000 track miles were approved for steam running, with seventeen locomotives approved for main line work, plus a number of potential locomotives coming on stream.

The sun is setting on 'Castle' 4-6-0 5051 *Drysllwyn Castle* as it heads the final outing of the GWS Great Western coaches on the main line, at Fenny Compton. 5051 left BR service in 1963 from Llanelli shed and it was taken to Barry Island where it became the fourth locomotive to depart from there in 1970. It arrived at GWS Didcot where it was overhauled to main line standards. 26 January 1980.

The light is fading as 5051 *Drysllwyn Castle* heads the Vintage Train at King's Sutton on the coaches' final main line journey to Didcot. 26 January 1980.

A new development in my railway enthusiasm heralded the start of sound recording steam locomotives in action. It was with considerable pleasure that 'A3' 4-6-2 4472 *Flying Scotsman* was my first recording. As you can imagine from the exhaust, the volume had been turned up as 4472 passed Clapham (Yorkshire) heading for Hellifield with the *Leander Limited* train. 26 April 1980.

A panoramic view
of Ribblehead
Viaduct in sunshine
as 'Jubilee' 4-6-0
5690 *Leander* heads
the *Leander Limited*
off the viaduct and
past the Blea Moor
Down Distant signal.
The train is destined
for Carlisle. 26 April
1980.

At about 5pm,
5690 *Leander* has
almost completed
the climb to Ais Gill
at Mallerstang in
good style, with the
return working of the
Leander Limited train
heading for Hellifield.
26 April 1980.

In sunshine, crowds of people eagerly anticipate the steam sections of the *Lancastrian* railtour. Their hopes were to be dashed by the fire risk requirements for a diesel pilot for all the steam stages of the tour. This involved 'Princess' 4-6-2 6201 *Princess Elizabeth* and 'Compound' 4-4-0 1000. Matters did not always run to plan. Here 6201 is at Chester. 17 May 1980.

An autumn holiday in Yorkshire gave an excellent opportunity to join the *CCE* at Carnforth and to travel to Seascale for a beach picnic. Before departing, there was time to visit Steamtown, Carnforth. In this picture, LMS 4-6-2 6201 *Princess Elizabeth* is viewing, with disdain, the southern interloper 'Lord Nelson' 4-6-0 850 *Lord Nelson*. The coaling tower is prominent. 2 September 1980.

'LN' 4-6-0 850 *Lord Nelson* is at Carnforth prior to working the *CCE*. The Maunsell designed locomotive appeared in August 1926 to provide motive power for the Southern Railway's 500 ton trains. After complaints of poor steaming, all the 'Nelsons' were fitted with a Lemaitre multiple jet exhaust and wide chimney, 850 being so treated in 1939. 850 was withdrawn in August 1962 and retained for the National Collection. It returned to steam and main line activity in 1980. 2 September 1980.

LMS 'Princess' 4-6-2 6201 *Princess Elizabeth* is taking the *CCE* away from the Seascale stop, towards its Sellafield destination, after an excellent run from Carnforth. 2 September 1980.

'Lord Nelson' 4-6-0 850 *Lord Nelson* enters Seascale station with the return working of the *CCE*. 850's exhaust sound provided an unusual eight beats per revolution of the driving wheels, instead of the customary four, in response to the 135 degree setting of the cranks. This arrangement was intended to give a more even torque and a more even draught on the fire. 2 September 1980.

Hiding partly behind a van are the sad looking remains of 'Jubilee' 4-6-0 45699 *Galatea*, observed from the *CCE* as it reached Carnforth. 45699 had been withdrawn from Shrewsbury shed in November 1964 and it eventually reached Barry in May 1965. It was rescued in 1980 and brought to Carnforth as a source of spares for sister *Leander*. Instead, *Galatea* has since been extensively restored and has performed superbly on main line work. 2 September 1980.

In autumn 1980, 6201 *Princess Elizabeth* was not often seen on the Settle to Carlisle line, but here she is powering the 450 ton *CME* to Ais Gill summit at 44 mph. Wild Boar Fell looks on. 4 September 1980.

Time for an infrastructure picture. Settle Junction signalbox is at rest, with no trains to disturb the peace. The door is open on this warm autumn day, where the view is looking north towards the junction. 13 September 1980.

A wet Open Day at Didcot Railway Centre was worthy of note, given the interesting visiting locomotives. In spite of the dismal weather, visitor 0-2-2 *Rocket* provided a bright appearance on this gloomy day. This replica of *Rocket* was built in 1979 by Locomotion Enterprises Limited for the 150th anniversary celebrations of the Rainhill Trials. 27 September 1980.

1910 Churchward designed 0-6-0 saddle tank 1363 spent most of its working life at Plymouth (Laira) shed, until withdrawal in January 1963. After storage at various locations, it eventually reached Didcot and is seen in steam on shed pilot duty. 27 September 1980.

Another visitor to Didcot was the National Collection's '9F' 2-10-0 92220 *Evening Star* where it was seen in steam. The '9F' had a working life of only five years and left service at Cardiff East Dock in March 1965. It was returned to steam in 1975 and carried out a number of main line duties. 27 September 1975.

Didcot's flagship locomotive 'Castle' 4-6-0 5051 *Drysllwyn Castle* was in steam on the same day. During its BR service, it carried the name *Earl Bathurst*. Always a pleasure to see, this well turned out locomotive last steamed in 2008 and is currently a static exhibit at Didcot. 27 September 1980.

'Manor' 4-6-0 7808 *Cookham Manor* was purchased direct from BR in 1965, having been withdrawn from Gloucester Horton Road shed. 7808 ceased steaming in 1983 but is seen here on the Didcot running line with GWR coaches behind the tender. 27 September 1980.

This is a main line bonus. The Leander Society special train from Saltley to Didcot was due to have 'Jubilee' motive power, but there was a last minute substitution with 'Ivatt 4MT' 2-6-0 43106 from the Severn Valley Railway. Here it is getting away strongly from Didcot on the return working. This locomotive left BR service in June 1968 and reached the SVR in August 1968. 27 September 1980.

A welcome return to the main line was made by Stanier 'Princess Coronation' 4-6-2 46229 *Duchess of Hamilton* in 1980. 46229 was withdrawn from Edge Hill in 1964 and purchased by Butlins soon after and displayed at Minehead. After restoration by the Friends of the National Railway Museum, 46229 ran on the main line between 1980 and 1996 as well as visiting preserved lines. In 1987 the locomotive was purchased by the National Railway Museum and in 2009 was restored to streamlined condition. It is now a static exhibit at NRM York. In this photo, 46229 waits in Carlisle to be attached to the southbound *CME*. 8 November 1980.

In the days of the Garsdale water stop, 46229 receives attention from her support crew before leaving for Hellifield with the southbound *CME*. 8 November 1980.

CHAPTER 6

1981: FROM SCOTLAND TO SCARBOROUGH AND A VERY OLD LOCOMOTIVE

In 1981, over 100 steam hauled specials were booked on the main line, a notable advance from 1972, but some warning signs were creeping in at the same time. There were some train cancellations due to lack of support and there was an increasing realisation of the growing costs of repairing steam locomotives. Nevertheless, there was a successful two day SLOA tour in Scotland, *The North Briton*, whilst two fresh locomotives graced the main line, namely Somerset & Dorset Joint Railway 2-8-0 '7F' 13809 and SR 'West Country' 4-6-2 34092 *City of Wells*.

Now that 'Princess Coronation' 46229 *Duchess of Hamilton* was back on the main line, viewing the locomotive from the lineside was the first attraction for 1981. Here it is stomping away from Ribblehead viaduct, northbound in appalling weather. 21 March 1981.

46229 is making steady progress towards Blea Moor at Ribblehead, with the northbound *Cumbrian Mountain Express* in pouring rain and strong winds typical of the area. 21 March 1981.

'LN' 4-6-0 850 *Lord Nelson* has completed its duty at Carnforth and was resting below the coaling tower, having worked the bottom leg of the *CME* from Hellifield. 21 March 1981.

A visit to the Bristol area in April 1981 enabled viewing of the *Welsh Marches Express* from the lineside. Here the sun is shining in the glorious countryside location of Llanvihangel bank as 'King' 4-6-0 6000 *King George V* steadily takes the *WME* northwards to Hereford, where steam traction will finish for the day. 18 April 1981.

Another view of 6000 as it forges up Llanvihangel bank, with the *WME* bound for its base at Hereford. 18 April 1981.

The introduction to this chapter referred to the *North Briton* railtour. This was a SLOA tour over two days in Scotland, with the first day's steam haulage behind 'A4' 4-6-2 60009 *Union of South Africa* from Mossend Yard to Perth, Dundee and back to Larbert. Number 9 as 60009 is known, was built at Doncaster in 1937 and ultimately became the last steam locomotive to be overhauled at Doncaster works, from where the 'A4' was allocated to Ferryhill shed, Aberdeen. The 'A4' was withdrawn in 1966 and shortly after purchased by John Cameron, and in May 1973 hauled its first main line excursion. Here it is at Gleneagles during a *North Briton* photostop. 9 May 1981.

This is definitely not a 'rivets' picture, but 60009 is heading the 'North Briton' away from Dundee on the Tay Bridge heading for Inverkeithing. The truncated supports for the original Tay Bridge are visible in the water to the left of the current bridge. 9 May 1981.

On day two of the *North Briton* railtour, steam haulage worked from Larbert and on to Edinburgh, Shotts and Mossend Yard. Motive power was double headed locomotives, North British 'J36' 0-6-0 673 *Maude* and LNER 'D49' 4-4-0 246 *Morayshire*. The 'D49' did not seem to be in the best of health with a steam leak on the right hand cylinder, but *Maude* was certainly working hard at times to compensate. Here the pair enters Larbert station at the beginning of the day's proceedings. 10 May 1981.

'D49' 246 is looking resplendent in LNER green at Larbert. It has appeared at preserved railways in this livery, and in BR black as 62712. 10 May 1981.

A misty photostop took place at Morningside Road on the Edinburgh suburban system with 673 and 246 adding their steam to the atmosphere. 673 was designed by Matthew Holmes and built in 1891. It was a First World War veteran, hence its naming after an army general of that era. The 0-6-0 lasted in BR service until 1966 and is now part of the Scottish Railway Preservation Society collection. It last saw action in 2002. 10 May 1981.

The *North Briton* double header is seen at Breich between Midcalder and Motherwell, prior to taking water. The mist gradually turned to fog, and this stop is in the latter stages of the journey to Mossend Yard, 10 May 1981.

A change of scenery and a first visit to the NYMR. The Lyke Wake Walk crosses the Yorkshire Moors from Osmotherley to Ravenscar and meets the NYMR at Fen Bog, which is near Goathland Summit. '4MT' 2-6-4T 80135 heads a train bound for Pickering. Built in 1956, 80135 spent a number of years at Plaistow shed on the London, Tilbury and Southend Railway system. It was withdrawn in August 1965 and spent seven years at Barry Island before being rescued for the NYMR. It was returned to steam in 1980 and carries BR green livery. 26 July 1981.

Back at York at about 7.30 pm, 'A3' 4-6-2 4472 *Flying Scotsman* is resplendent in the evening sun as it backs into Leeman Road sidings after working a train from Carnforth. 26 July 1981.

A couple of days later, 4472 has worked the *Scarborough Spa Express* from York to Scarborough and return. It is waiting to return to the depot at York after its working. Note how small an audience it attracts in comparison to modern day occasions. 28 July 1981.

The Mid Hants Railway was the next steam destination, particularly to travel behind a Maunsell 2-6-0, which were my firm favourites after seeing them on the Reading to Redhill line. 'U' 2-6-0 31806 was in steam and provided haulage from Alresford to Ropley, then the extent of the running line. 31806 was withdrawn from Guildford shed in January 1964 and languished at Barry before returning to steam at the MHR in 1981. 1 August 1981.

Not every rescued locomotive from Barry was restored straightaway, and at the MHR, Maunsell 'U' 2-6-0 31625 was no exception. After ceasing BR service in January 1964 from Guildford shed, 31625 spent sixteen years at Barry Island before reaching the MHR in 1980 and later being returned to steam. I had the privilege of a footplate experience on this locomotive at the MHR, before it moved to the Swanage Railway, where it once more waits restoration. 1 August 1981.

Also active at the MHR was rebuilt 'West Country' 4-6-2 34016 *Bodmin,* seen here entering Ropley with a train from Alresford. 34016 had served BR until June 1964 when it too went to Barry until 1972. It commenced restoration at Quainton Road in Buckinghamshire but moved to the MHR in 1976 to be returned to steam in 1980. 34016 has since moved to Carnforth, where it awaits further attention. 1 August 1981.

Now away to the other end of the UK, to the Strathspey Railway, where Stanier 'Black 5' 4-6-0 5025 was in action. Built in 1934, 5025 is the oldest surviving example of its class. It was withdrawn from Carnforth in August 1968, at the end of BR steam, and went to the Keighley & Worth Valley Railway before relocating to Aviemore, Here, 5025 is running round its train at Boat of Garten. 5 September 1981.

This photograph depicts 5025 and Boat of Garten station on a pleasant summer afternoon. The train is ready to depart for Aviemore. The locomotive has subsequently been subject of an in-depth overhaul and has freshly returned to steam in 2021. 5 September 1981.

The GWS held an October open day at Didcot where two guest locomotives were in action. '9F' 2-10-0 92220 *Evening Star* is slowly moving towards the turntable. 10 October 1981.

The star of the event at Didcot was the 1838 0-4-2 *Lion*, built by Todd, Kitson and Laird for the London & Manchester Railway. After its railway service, it was used as a dock stationary pumping engine until rescued by the LMSR. *Lion* had various film appearances and was overhauled at the Vulcan Works of Ruston Diesels Ltd for the 1980 'Rocket 150' celebrations. It is depicted at Didcot hauling appropriate carriages on the branch line near Radstock Halt. 10 October 1981.

GWR '14XX' 0-4-2T 1466 was on duty at Didcot with autotrailer 231 and awaited its next call to action. This locomotive was purchased from BR in 1964 and formed the foundation of the GWS. It is currently under overhaul with the prospect of steaming soon, although it had been hoped for a return in 2021, the 60th year of the Society. 10 October 1981.

A fresh locomotive to experience on the *Cumbrian Mountain* trains was 'West Country' Pacific 34092 *City of Wells*. 34092 had been withdrawn in 1964 and languished at Barry until 1971 when it became the first Bulleid Pacific to leave the yard. Returned to steam in 1980, it was on the Carnforth to Hellifield leg of the *CMP* on this occasion. 34092 is seen at Carnforth overshadowed by the coaling tower. 28 November 1981.

In the early days of main line steam excursions, 'run pasts' were a regular feature and 34092 is performing a run past at Wennington station with the *CMP*, which it will eventually take to Hellifield. 28 November 1981.

Engine change for the *CMP* took place at Hellifield, where 'A4' 4-6-2 4498 *Sir Nigel Gresley* is about to take its place at the head of the train. In those days, it seemed to be accepted that the participants would photograph the locomotive at Hellifield and 4498 is nicely illuminated by the winter sun. 28 November 1981.

CHAPTER 7

1982: THE YEAR OF NUMBER ONE

In spite of the concerns raised in 1981, trains for 1982 were loading well. Excursion traffic was mainly to be found on the Settle to Carlisle and Welsh Marches routes, whilst the Trans Pennine route was deleted from the programmes. The specials traffic continued during the year in such a way that it prompted BR to announce that steam hauled trains would continue until 1990. There was also general realisation that fares had to increase to cover costs.

For its first two runs over the Settle to Carlisle line, 'King Arthur' 4-6-0 777 *Sir Lamiel* was obliged to have 'Black 5' 4-6-0 5407 coupled to the train to assist 777 if required. Nevertheless, 777 put in some hard work and soon proved its capability, enabling some excellent solo performances on special trains. *Sir Lamiel* had been withdrawn from BR service in October 1961 from Basingstoke shed and was earmarked for preservation in the National Collection. Restoration started in 1978. After three periods of being in steam between 1982 and 2017, the locomotive is awaiting a decision on its future at Loughborough on the GCR. 777 is depicted in front of 5407 at Carlisle before taking the southbound *CMP* to Hellifield. 3 April 1982.

Here is an action picture of 777 *Sir Lamiel* piloting 'Black 5' 5407 at Armathwaite, whilst performing a run past. It was a delight to be able to see the locomotives in action as well as riding behind them. Today's tour operators, please note. 3 April 1982.

SDJR '7F' 2-8-0 as LMS 13809, is depicted bringing the empty stock of the *CMP* into Hellifield station. This train will form the 'bottom leg' of the tour brought to Hellifield by 777 & 5407. 13809 was built in 1925 by Robert Stephenson & Co. Ltd and worked mainly between Bath and Bournemouth until withdrawal in June 1964. It became the 78th locomotive to leave Barry scrapyard and returned to steam in 1980. On the journey from Hellifield to Carnforth, 13809 was driven by Charlie Fothergill, who proceeded to drive the 2-8-0 with great gusto, achieving 60 mph downhill and thrashing so hard uphill that I thought the 2-8-0 would be harmed. Not a bit of it! 3 April 1982.

Above left: Dinting Railway Centre was opened in 1968, using an ex-Manchester, Sheffield & Lincolnshire Railway shed to house 'Jubilee' 4-6-0 5596 *Bahamas*. It provided a base for other locomotives from time to time, and 'A2' Pacific 532 *Blue Peter* is seen here under cover from the elements. 532 did not return to the main line until 1992. 10 April 1982.

Above right: Amongst the other occupants of the Dinting shed was 'A4' (600)19 *Bittern* in a red lead paint covering. *Bittern* was withdrawn in September 1966, being one of the last two 'A4's in service. Currently, it is owned by Locomotive Services Ltd and is in store after a period of excellent main line performances where speeds in excess of 90mph were achieved. 10 April 1982.

Right: At the time of this Dinting visit, the LNWR was represented by 2-4-0 790 *Hardwicke* and 'Coal Tank' 0-6-2T 1054. In this picture, *Hardwicke* is looking from the shed to the open spaces. 10 April 1982.

Above left: LNWR 'Coal Tank' 1054 was fortuitously placed outside Dinting Shed. It ended its service in 1958 and was purchased by the National Trust, initially for display at Penrhyn Castle. For a period around the 1980 *Rocket150* celebrations, it was maintained in main line running condition at Dinting. It is currently based at the KWVR. 10 April 1982.

Above right: Lancashire & Yorkshire Railway 0-6-0 saddle tank 752 is in steam at Haworth on the KWVR, during its first steaming season in preservation. It was rebuilt from an 0-6-0 tender engine in 1896 and ultimately survived in service with the Coal Board until 1968. 752 has been recently restored to steam once more and is based at the East Lancashire Railway. 3 May 1982.

Left: For over fifty years, this popular '4F' 0-6-0 43924 has been based at the KWVR. It was built in 1920 by the Midland Railway and its last main line shed was Bristol (Barrow Road) from where it was withdrawn in 1965. 43924 went to Barry Island and became the first locomotive to depart for preservation. 3 May 1982.

Two locomotives exemplifying the extent of our nation's railway heritage assets were to be seen at the preserved GCR in Summer 1982. Firstly, Great Central Railway 'Improved Director' 4-4-0 506 *Butler Henderson* is in steam at Loughborough. Built at Gorton in 1919, 506 served until 1960 when it was withdrawn from Sheffield Darnall shed. As an engine from the National Collection, it steamed on the preserved GCR from 1982 to 1999. 12 June 1982.

The second attraction at the GCR in summer 1982 was the 'Stirling Single', Great Northern Railway No. 1. Built at Doncaster in 1870 and withdrawn in 1907, this 4-2-2 with 8ft driving wheels was successful in hauling express trains in Victorian times. Incredibly, it was restored to steam in 1981 and spent some time in 1982 working at the GCR. Here No. 1 gets away from Loughborough with a train for Rothley. 12 June 1982.

No. 1 presents an impression of speed and elegance as it heads south on the GCR at Kinchley Lane. A splendid opportunity to witness a heritage machine in operation. 12 June 1982.

The 'Stirling Single' makes an impressive start from Quorn as it heads for Rothley on the GCR. It was a pleasure to ride behind this venerable machine and listen to the well-spaced exhaust beats in response to the turning of the huge driving wheels. 12 June 1982.

As a matter of record, BR '8P' 4-6-2 71000 *Duke of Gloucester* was on view at Loughborough during its restoration at the GCR. Clearly there is much work to do before its recommissioning in November 1986. 12 June 1982.

Currently, Tyseley Locomotive Works is much in the railway news after seventy years of activity in preservation. One of the 'Castle' locomotives based there, 7029 *Clun Castle* is at speed passing King's Sutton with the *Salopian* heading for Dorridge. It has returned to steam in 2019 after a heavy general overhaul at Tyseley. I was fortunate to travel on the railtour hauled by *Clun Castle* celebrating fifty years since the return of main line steam on 2 October 2021. 19 June 1982.

By contrast, 'Castle' 4-6-0 5080 *Defiant* stands forlornly at Tyseley as it awaits restoration. 5080 was completed at Swindon works in 1939 and spent the majority of its working life based at South Wales sheds, being withdrawn from Llanelli shed in April 1963. After nearly eleven years at Barry, it was taken to Tyseley and returned to steam in 1987. 10 July 1982.

A visit to the SVR was long overdue and on a fine July day 'Hall' 4-6-0 4930 *Hagley Hall* has just arrived at Bridgnorth with the 4.15pm train from Bewdley. The 1929 built 4-6-0 worked for thirty-four years achieving a service of 1.25 million miles. After a spell at Barry Island, 4930 arrived at the SVR in 1973 and returned to steam in 1979. It participated in a number of main line tours and worked at the SVR until 1986. It is currently being restored for the next stage of its career. 10 July 1982.

The sun illuminates the paintwork of '2251' 0-6-0 3205 at Bridgnorth. This Collett designed 0-6-0 was built in 1946 and was purchased from BR in 1965. It moved from the DVR to the SVR to work the latter's first passenger service on 23 May 1970. Now back at the DVR, 3205 awaits overhaul. 10 July 1982.

Didcot's 'Castle' 4-6-0 5051 *Drysllwyn Castle* was the motive power for the *Devonian* railtour. The load was eight coaches and the weather dry. The route took the train from Didcot to Leamington Spa and on to Stratford Upon Avon where 5051 is pictured. On the return run from Leamington Spa southwards, Driver Archie Davis certainly had the regulator wide open, judging by the huge sound effects. 9 October 1982.

A birthday found my wife and me on the thirteen coach *WMP* hauled by 'Duchess' 4-6-2 46229 *Duchess of Hamilton* between Newport and Shrewsbury. At Hereford, we were treated to three runpasts, with 46229 performing nicely. Next to the tender is the preserved LNWR Royal Brake vehicle. 31 October 1982.

Before winter set in too strongly, a linesiding trip occurred in November to see the *CMP* in action. 'Black 5' 4-6-0 5407 is storming away from Wennington as it heads for Hellifield. 5407 was an Armstrong Whitworth product of 1937 and it worked until the end of steam in 1968. Now owned by Ian Riley, it is a regular main line performer, especially between Fort William and Mallaig. 27 November 1982.

CHAPTER 8

1983: DOUBLE HEADINGS AND A SPECIAL 60TH BIRTHDAY

At the beginning of another year, there was a full programme of trains for SLOA. One highlight of 1983 was the double heading of 'Midland Compound' 1000 and 'Jubilee' 5690 *Leander*, over the Settle to Carlisle line, in a blizzard, of which more, later in this chapter. In spite of the success of steam hauled trains over the Settle to Carlisle line, BR announced its intention to close the line. The ensuing story is well known and the now much used line is thankfully still with us.

During the year, it was made clear that more stringent inspection procedures would be needed for steam locomotives, with the corresponding increase in ticket prices to follow. The increases were understandable, given that ticket prices had been kept low by various forms of subsidy, including the input by volunteers.

William Shakespeare trains appeared for the first time from Paddington to Stratford Upon Avon, including steam power from Didcot to Stratford.

A bright day in the New Year beckoned a visit to Didcot Railway Centre. On the running line, 'Pannier Tank' 0-6-0PT 3738 is toying with its small load of two coaches. 3738 spent most of its career initially in the London area and latterly in South Wales. Withdrawn from Cardiff East Dock in 1965, it was then stored at Barry. It was released in April 1974 and has since been through three boiler tickets. It is now a static exhibit. 2 January 1983.

Also basking in the sun at Didcot was '53XX' 2-6-0 5322. It is always a pleasure for me to see GWR Moguls as they regularly worked over the Reading to Redhill line, close to my first home. 5322 was Swindon built in 1917 and saw overseas service in France with the Railway Operating Division of the Army. Its final posting was at Pontypool Road shed from where it was withdrawn in 1965. In 1969, it became the third locomotive to leave Barry Island. The '53XX' has worked at Didcot and appeared on some preserved lines, steaming finally in 2014. Its firebox problems await resolution. 2 January 1983.

With this picture, we pay tribute to Bernard Staite, who did so much to support SLOA and organise railtours for many years. He is sadly no longer with us, but a huge debt of gratitude is due to him from lovers of steam. Wennington. 5 February 1983.

Double heading on the bottom leg of the *CMP* is necessary with a fourteen coach train. The scene is at Wennington, where 'K1' 2-6-0 2005 and 'Black 5' 4-6-0 5407 perform a run past, an enjoyable feature of early railtours. 5 February 1983.

The *CMP* of 5 February 1983 had a huge surprise waiting in the sky. At Hellifield, the picture is of 'Midland Compound' 4-4-0 1000 and 'Jubilee' 5690 *Leander* backing down the yard to replenish water supplies. There was no sign of the blizzard that would ensue over the Long Drag, and the train ran straight through to Appleby, where there was no snow. That was the end of the steam section, but the two locomotives and crews had done sterling work to get safely to Appleby. 5 February 1983.

Having travelled behind 1000 and 5690 on 5 February, the southbound *CMP* behind the same locomotives just had to be seen from the lineside and we were not disappointed as the classic pairing climbs from Mallerstang towards Ais Gill summit, in a snowscape. 12 February 1983.

A closer view of the two locomotives working to Ais Gill. It is clear that the 'Compound' is doing its share of the work. My abiding memory is of the elegant big wheeled movement of the 'Compound' and the shuffling three cylinder exhaust of the 'Jubilee' behind the 4-4-0. A legendary sight and a treasured experience. 12 February 1983.

One of the runs to celebrate the sixtieth anniversary of Gresley Pacific 'A3' 4472 *Flying Scotsman* was from Peterborough to York. To salute this venerable machine, we journeyed to Stoke Bank to see 4472 near Burton Coggles. 27 February 1983.

Another visit to Dinting Railway Centre found LNER 'A2' 4-6-2 532 *Blue Peter* in steam. The 'A2' was not ready for the main line, but looked the part, in steam. Doncaster built in 1948, it was withdrawn in December 1966 and purchased by Geoff Drury. 532 had a number of main line turns and preserved line duties, ceasing in 2002. It is now being overhauled at Crewe, in the ownership of Jeremy Hosking. 2 April 1983.

Travelling on the *WMP* was an enjoyable spring event for 1983. Steam power for the Shrewsbury to Hereford section was provided by 'Castle' 4-6-0 5051 *Drysllwyn Castle* and a rousing run ensued. Here 5051 is powering through Craven Arms during a run past, whilst GWR lower quadrant signals guard the route. 9 April 1983.

5051 relinquished the *WMP* at Hereford to 'King Arthur' 4-6-0 777 *Sir Lamiel*. 777 was in charge of the Hereford to Newport and return sections of the journey. The picture shows the 4-6-0 backing through Newport station to turn on the nearby triangle before returning to Hereford. 9 April 1983.

A visit was paid to Keighley, when returning home from Yorkshire. Unexpectedly, SDJR '7F' 2-8-0 13809 was present as it awaited the call to work a *CMP*. 2 May 1983.

A 'King' 4-6-0, but not as you would expect to see it. 6024 *King Edward I* was in process of a lengthy restoration at the Buckinghamshire Railway Centre at Quainton. The working conditions must have been bleak in winter. 6024 had been at Barry since 1962 and was rescued in 1973, to be returned to steam in 1989. After much main line work, it is currently under restoration for Jeremy Hosking. 30 May 1983.

On the SVR, 'Manor' 4-6-0 7812 *Erlestoke Manor* enters Bridgnorth with a train from Bewdley. From a small class of thirty engines, nine 'Manors' survive in preservation. 7812 was completed at Swindon in 1939 and worked in the West Midlands, the West Country and finally in Wales for working the *Cambrian Coast Express*. After eight years at Barry, it reached the SVR to enter service in 1979. 19 June 1983.

Two years after my previous visit, the MHR beckoned again; the motive power for the journey between Four Marks and Alresford was 'U' 2-6-0 31806, which looked in good fettle in the sunshine at Alresford. 13 August 1983.

Also in steam at the MHR was Maunsell 'N' 2-6-0 31874. The 'N' spent the majority of its career at Bricklayers Arms shed and would have visited the Reading to Redhill line many times. 31874 is presently being restored at the Swanage Railway. Here it is leaving Ropley, tender first, for Medstead & Four Marks. 13 August 1983.

Dugald Drummond designed 4-4-0 'T9' 30120 was built by the London & South Western Railway at Nine Elms in 1899. The good performance of the 'T9's earned them the nickname 'Greyhounds', and all the class reached BR service. By 1961, they had all been withdrawn except 30120 which was overhauled at Eastleigh Works and painted in LSWR colours as number 120. As part of the National Collection, it was then on loan to the MHR, pending steaming. 13 August 1983.

On return from holiday in Scotland, a brief visit was paid to Beamish Museum. Here North Eastern Railway 0-6-0 876 in NER livery is at rest, coupled to a complementary clerestory coach. The BR class 'J21' 0-6-0 has been grant funded for restoration and is currently at Locomotion, Shildon. 3 September 1983.

Flying Scotsman in Scotland, with the *Fair Maid* railtour, was a tempting prospect in spite of a very early start. The 'A3' started from Mossend yard, thence to Stirling, Perth, Newburgh, Ladybank, Forth Bridge and finishing at Edinburgh Waverley. A long day but enjoyable. 4472 is seen here at the Gleneagles photo stop. 1 October 1983.

The final rail activity for 1983 was to lineside 'West Country' 4-6-2 34092 *City of Wells* as it worked the *CMP* between Leeds and Carlisle. The 4-6-2 was built at Brighton Works and soon became a regular on boat trains between Victoria and the Channel Ports. 34092 then moved to Salisbury and was withdrawn from there in 1964. First based at the KWVR, it is now resident at the East Lancashire Railway. Main line activity in preservation took place on the Settle to Carlisle line and between Marylebone and Stratford Upon Avon. This scene shows 34092 approaching Hellifield. 3 December 1983.

CHAPTER 9

1984: STEAM TO MALLAIG AND A GWR 4-4-0

Exciting events for 1984 were marked particularly by the introduction of steam special trains on the Fort William to Mallaig line. As we now know, their popularity has certainly not diminished and the trains still fill to capacity. Stanier 'Black 5' locomotives 5407 and 44767 were the main performers, with 'J36' 0-6-0 *Maude* appearing on a few runs to Glenfinnan. However, there were some signs of poor loadings even on the *Cumbrian Mountain* trains, whilst fire risks during the summer caused some diesel hauled replacements. The preserved lines continued to prosper, with freshly restored engines appearing and passenger numbers increasing. The movement was certainly maturing.

On a very cold February day, the *CME* hauled by 'Duchess' 4-6-2 46229 *Duchess of Hamilton* was the attraction. It produced the fastest time from Hellifield to Blea Moor in preservation, to date, with a thirteen coach load. 46229 is backing towards the coaching stock at Hellifield. 4 February 1984.

Once again the schedule permitted runpasts at Appleby, where 46229 produced some explosive performances to the delight of the audience. 4 February 1984.

'Black 5' 4-6-0 44767 *George Stephenson* had worked the Carnforth to Hellifield section of the *CME* on 4 February and it was going well on Giggleswick Bank a week later, heading for Carnforth. 44767 was the last LMS built steam locomotive, under the aegis of H.G. Ivatt, who introduced Stephenson Link valve gear to this locomotive. 11 February 1984.

This is the first year that 'A4' 4-6-2 60009 *Union of South Africa* had been seen south of the Scottish border, since returning to steam in 1971. 60009 was withdrawn from Aberdeen Ferryhill shed in summer 1966 and was then acquired by John Cameron. This much respected 'A4' has recently run for the last time, before retiring to Mr Cameron's farm. Here it is in full chat with the southbound *CME* at Long Marton. 31 March 1984.

The headboard has changed, and 60009 is still looking resplendent at Hellifield, after relinquishing the *CME* coaches. 31 March 1984.

This was the 150th locomotive to leave Barry Island. It is a worthy reminder of the condition of some of the projects that left there, and it is so good to see 'Hall' 4-6-0 4953 *Pitchford Hall* working well currently. This view is at Norchard on the Dean Forest Railway where 4953's restoration had started earlier in the year. 16 April 1984.

Whilst emitting a pall of black smoke would incur displeasure today, SDJR 2-8-0 13809 is battling towards Hellifield with the northbound *CME* at Keerholme. 13809 was making steady progress in spite of the exhaust. 21 April 1984.

'9F' 2-10-0 92220 *Evening Star* was the last steam locomotive to be built at Swindon, and the last for BR, in 1960. It worked in the Cardiff area and later on the SDJR in 1962 and 1963. After withdrawal it was renovated at Crewe and is part of the National Collection. Its last steaming was in 1989 and it is in action here at Ribblehead Viaduct, heading for Carlisle. 21 April 1984.

LNWR 'Super D' 0-8-0 49395 left BR service in 1959 after thirty-eight years' work. It was originally planned for inclusion in a Leicester Museum, but that plan changed. After various storage locations, the 0-8-0 moved in 1981 to the Telford Industrial Museum at Blists Hill as shown here. 23 June 1984.

The branch from Axminster to Lyme Regis closed in 1965, having been home to three members of the '0415' class 4-4-2T's, designed by William Adams and built in 1885. This Adams Radial Tank arrived under its own steam at the Bluebell Railway for preservation in 1961 and was restored to LSWR livery as number 488. It has made occasional appearances in BR livery as 30583, as seen here. 14 July 1984.

The Bluebell Railway also became home for a modern locomotive in the shape of BR '4MT' 4-6-0 75027, which had a working career of fourteen years, before withdrawal in August 1968. In 1969 it reached the Bluebell Railway and is seen here hauling a Sheffield Park to Horsted Keynes train near Freshfield. 14 July 1984.

The chapter introduction mentions the Fort William to Mallaig steam trains, and a summer holiday at Morar facilitated linesiding and riding on the train. 'Black 5' 5407 is pictured departing Morar for Mallaig on a bright sunny day, as the sound of the locomotive echoes from the cutting. 19 August 1984.

This is 'Black 5' 4-6-0 44767 climbing to Glenfinnan Summit from the stop at Glenfinnan Station, with a Mallaig bound train. Six coaches was the load limit at the time, and blue and grey livery ruled. 22 August 1984.

An on-train view at Morar level crossing where, in 1984, the gates had to be opened by the train guard. 44767 is the motive power and it will have to wait for the guard to rejoin the train. 23 August 1984.

This railway is no longer with us. The Isle of Mull Railway opened in 1983 and ran from Craignure Harbour Station to Torosay, the stop for the Torosay Hotel. *Lady of the Isles* 2-6-4T is shown awaiting departure from Craignure. This 10¼ inch gauge line closed in 2010 and the track was lifted in 2012. 28 August 1984.

The main line beckoned when the GWS promoted the *Jubilee Castle* train between Didcot and Kidderminster, as well as a run on the SVR with 'Modified Hall' 6960 *Raveningham Hall*. Main line motive power on the outward run was 'Jubilee' 4-6-0 5690 *Leander*, seen in early autumn light at Didcot. 6 October 1984.

Above left: A stranger to Didcot. 'A1X' 0-6-0T 32670 from the Kent & East Sussex Railway was in evidence. Built at Brighton in 1872, this hard-working survivor joined the KESR as No. 3 *Bodiam* in 1901 and continued into the BR era. Now part of the preserved KESR fleet, 32670 is currently under repair at the NNR. 6 October 1984.

Above right: George Jackson Churchward followed William Dean as Locomotive Superintendent of the GWR in 1902, and during 1903 his new 'City' class 4-4-0's were being delivered. This one is 3440 *City of Truro*, whose claimed top speed of 102.3mph in May 1904, still causes endless debate. By 1931, *City of Truro's* career was at an end, but it was preserved to be kept at the new York Railway Museum. In 1957, it was restored to working order and hauled special and service trains until 1961. In 1984, it was taken to Bridgnorth for restoration and use in the *GW150* celebrations of 1985. As 3717, the locomotive awaits refurbishment at Bridgnorth. 29 October 1984.

This view of Bridgnorth shed in 1984 shows how the SVR has matured. The line-up includes Ivatt '4MT' 2-6-0 43106; pioneer locomotive '2251' 0-6-0 3205; 'Black 5' 4-6-0 5000, a member of the National Collection; lastly 'Modified Hall' 4-6-0 6960 *Raveningham Hall* which had a preservation career on the SVR and the West Somerset Railway before recently becoming part of the Jeremy Hosking fleet. 29 October 1984.

A pleasant November facilitated viewing the *WME* which required two locomotives allocated on the day. Far from its regular haunts, 'Merchant Navy' 4-6-2 35028 *Clan Line* attacks the grade to Leebotwood and leaves a clean exhaust in its wake. 10 November 1984.

35028's colleague on the *WME.* was 'Modified Hall' 6960 *Raveningham Hall* which is strenuously attacking the grade to Llanvihangel Station as it heads for Pontypool. 10 November 1984.

The story of the purchase of GWR '14XX' 0-4-2T 1466 is well known, and this first purchase for the Great Western Society laid the foundation for the superb collection of locomotives at Didcot. 1466 is in steam at Didcot, coupled to an autocoach. 9 December 1984.

CHAPTER 10

1985: GW150 AND MARYLEBONE STEAM

985 was a year of considerable steam activity, as the 150th anniversary of the founding of the GWR was marked by events throughout the year. January 1985 saw the forerunner of the Marylebone to Stratford Upon Avon trains in the shape of the *Thames-Avon Express*. The ensuing Sunday Lunch trains loaded well and ran successfully with an initial allocation of Pacific locomotives.

The opening GW150 train from Bristol to Plymouth in April encountered hot axle box problems on the outward run, but after strenuous repair efforts, ran well on the return. In August, GW150 trains were run successfully between Swindon and Gloucester with a three locomotive stud based at Horton Road, Gloucester. Celebrations were enhanced by the efforts made by preserved railways' volunteers.

Meanwhile, a 'Duchess' Pacific put in some rousing record breaking performances on the climb out of High Wycombe to Saunderton.

The sun glints on the paintwork of 'A4' 4498 *Sir Nigel Gresley* as it heads for Stratford-upon-Avon with the first *Thames-Avon Express* from Marylebone. This is the forerunner of the successful Marylebone to Stratford Sunday lunch trains. The location is Bradenham, just north of High Wycombe. 26 January 1985.

Would that the sun had shone at this location! It is pouring with rain as 'Manor' 4-6-0 7819 *Hinton Manor* approaches Whiteball Tunnel mouth, with the inaugural GW150 special to Plymouth from Bristol. Sadly, the 'Manor' only reached Exeter before succumbing to a hot axlebox. 7 April 1985.

The return GW150 special to Bristol was double headed by 'Hall' 4-6-0 4930 *Hagley Hall* and 'Manor' 7819 *Hinton Manor*. Overnight work by support crews had restored the running ability of the 'Manor' and, coupled to the 'Hall', it had a trouble free run. Here the pair are in full flight past Chelvey, en route for Bristol. 8 April 1985.

'King' 4-6-0 6023 *King Edward II* was completed at Swindon in June 1930 and towards the end of its working life went to Cardiff Canton shed in 1960, before withdrawal in 1962. It went to Barry in that year and finally departed in 1984, having sustained cut driving wheels. As the signage in the photograph explains, 6023 was purchased by Harvey's of Bristol, to enable restoration by the Brunel Trust to commence. This work was not completed, but Didcot Railway Centre purchased the 'King' and it was restored to steam in 2011. 8 April 1985.

'Merchant Navy' 4-6-2 35028 *Clan Line* soon participated in the Marylebone to Stratford Upon Avon trains and is seen here at the head of the *Thames-Avon Express* at Saunderton summit on the outward run. A footpath crosses the line here, providing a useful vantage point. 13 April 1985.

'Duchess' Pacific 46229 became a regular performer on the Marylebone to Stratford trains and is seen making good progress in Saunderton cutting, where the up and down lines separate, with the return train to Marylebone. 12 May 1985.

Didcot's attractions for GW150 included recently restored '52XX' 2-8-0T 5224. This had been refurbished at the GCR, by 1984, six years after its sojourn at Barry had ended. 5224's working career was mostly in South Wales until withdrawal in 1963. It is heading the Travelling Post Office coaches on Didcot's running line. 29 May 1985.

This replica of GWR Broad Gauge 4-2-2 *Iron Duke* was completed in 1985 for the 'GW150' celebrations. It is a National Railway Museum asset and has been based at Didcot since 2013. It has not been steamed since the early 1990s. In this picture, it is being carried on a well wagon. 29 May 1985.

The sole preserved, 1938 built, 'Dukedog' 4-4-0 was another exhibit at Didcot's 'GW150' exhibition. Shown here as 3217 *Earl of Berkeley*, it was not in steam on this occasion. Normally based at the Bluebell Railway, it was last steamed in 2011, having briefly worked at the Llangollen Railway wearing BR black livery as 9017. 29 May 1985.

Meanwhile, back at Saunderton summit, a tremendous power output had been made by 'Duchess' 46229 *Duchess of Hamilton*. With a train loading of 430 tons, the 4-6-2 had roared to the summit, from a standing start at High Wycombe, topping the bank at 73mph and developing over 3,500hp, a new record. Although I did not witness this event on 26 May 1985, I did see 46229 in similar action on 29 June, when it was being worked very hard to Saunderton summit. The 'wuuummmph' as it roared under the bridge at Saunderton Lea had to be heard to be believed. I had the privilege of corresponding with driver Gordon Read, who had worked the record breaking train. 29 June 1985.

The GW150 activities continued with a main line tour, the *Western Stalwart*, which was to have had *City of Truro* and two 'Castle' locomotives as motive power. In the event, 'Hall' 4930 *Hagley Hall* and 'Castle' 7029 *Clun Castle* double headed the train for the steam sections. During the afternoon, I learned I had won the raffled headboard! In this picture, 4930 and 7029 drift into Abergavenny during a photostop. 6 July 1985.

Further GW150 activity took place in August, when steam hauled trains were run between Swindon and Gloucester. 'Castle' 4-6-0 5051 *Drysllwyn Castle* is seen near Frampton Crossing, struggling on the climb to Sapperton, with a Swindon bound train. 5051 was later under repair at Gloucester. 11 August 1985.

The smaller 4-6-0's in the team of GWR locomotives for the Swindon to Gloucester trains seemed to be more at ease, as exemplified by 'Hall' 4930 *Hagley Hall* on the westbound climb to Sapperton at Hailey Wood. 11 August 1985.

'Manor' 4-6-0
7819 *Hinton Manor*
seemed in good fettle
at Tarlton, on the
climb to Sapperton,
with a Gloucester
bound train. All the
locomotives were
well presented for
this series of trains.
13 August 1985.

Gloucester Horton
Road shed. The
GWR line-up at
85B comprises
7819, 5051, and
4930 in that order,
as they rest after
their exertions with
the Swindon to
Gloucester special
'GW150' trains.
15 August 1985.

GWR '38XX' 2-8-0 3822 was built in 1940 and was based in South Wales for all of its service life, although it did reach other parts of the GWR system. It was withdrawn from Cardiff East Dock and soon arrived at Barry, leaving for Didcot in May 1976. It was returned to steam at Didcot just in time for the GW150 celebrations and is seen here at Didcot, attached to a Siphon G parcels van. 28 September 1985.

A final view of GW150 activity. On the SVR, 'City' 4-4-0 3440 *City of Truro* heads for Arley with a Bewdley train, at Severn Lodge. The autumn sunshine gently highlights the livery of this delightful National Collection treasure. 29 September 1985.

Away from the main line, 'Terriers' are at work on the KESR. Back-to-back, double headed 'Terriers' create a spectacle as they leave Rolvenden and start the climb to Tenterden Station. 32670 is the long term KESR locomotive, whilst 10, in green livery, is here named *Sutton* to respect the support given by the Borough of Sutton in her restoration. 26 October 1985.

As the autumn light fades, the 'Terriers' are in action on another run at Tenterden bank as they leave Rolvenden. 32670 is leading 10 *Sutton*. The sound of these two locomotives working hard could be heard for some while in the still, late afternoon air. 26 October 1985.

On a bright December day, 'A4' 4498 *Sir Nigel Gresley* leaves Bicester North with a Stratford-upon-Avon train from Marylebone. The sunlight provides excellent lighting for the whole locomotive, especially illuminating the wheels and motion. 7 December 1985.

'A3' 4472 *Flying Scotsman* is in action with a *William Shakespeare* train bound for Stratford-upon-Avon. It is seen at Saunderton in dwindling winter light. No crowds here on such occasions, unlike the present day. 29 December 1985.

EPILOGUE

It has been a pleasure and an exercise full of interest, and some surprises, to bring this collection of Steam Heritage pictures together for this book. It is interesting to note that Gresley Pacifics appeared very early in Chapter One and again in the final chapter. The preservation movement was growing in stature, not only on the main line, but also on preserved lines as shown by the incredible diversity of motive power illustrated. Do please remember that the events of 1972 took place half a century before the time of writing this book, and steam is still going strong. There is much of interest to report in the period 1986 to 2000 and a sequel to *Steam Heritage 1972 to 1985* is intended to cover these years in the not too distant future.

Floreat Vapor, and huge thanks to all who work with Steam.

GLOSSARY

BR	British Railways
CCE (P)	Cumbrian Coast Express (Pullman)
CME(P)	Cumbrian Mountain Express (Pullman)
DVR	Dart Valley Railway
GCR	Great Central Railway
GNR	Great Northern Railway
GWR	Great Western Railway
GWS	Great Western Society
KESR	Kent & East Sussex Railway
KWVR	Keighley & Worth Valley Railway
LMS	London Midland & Scottish Railway
LNER	London & North Eastern Railway
LNWR	London & North Western Railway
LSWR	London & South Western Railway
LT	London Transport
MGNJRPS	Midland & Great Northern Joint Railway Preservation Society
MHR	Mid Hants Railway
MNLPS	Merchant Navy Locomotive Preservation Society
MR	Midland Railway
MRC	Midland Railway Centre
NER	North Eastern Railway
NNR	North Norfolk Railway
NRM	National Railway Museum
NYMR	North Yorkshire Moors Railway
RER	Ravenglass & Eskdale Railway
SDJR	Somerset & Dorset Joint Railway
SDR	South Devon Railway
SLOA	Steam Locomotive Operators Association
SR	Southern Railway
SVR	Severn Valley Railway
WME(P)	Welsh Marches Express (Pullman)

BIBLIOGRAPHY

Britain's Preserved Locomotives, Steam Railway, 2019
Rail 150 Exhibition Steam Cavalcade Guide Book, 1975
SHARMAN, Bill, *Main Line Steam,* Atlantic 1997
Steam Locomotive Operators' Association Guide Book, SLOA, 1980
WARREN, Alan, *Barry Scrapyard,* David & Charles 1988
WHITELEY J.E. and MORRISON G.W., *Preserved Steam on the Main Line,* OPC 1989